IN A BEAUTIFUL COUNTRY

Kevin Prufer

Four Way Books
Tribeca

Please direct all inquiries to:
Editorial Office
Four Way Books
POB 535, Village Station
New York, NY 10014
www.fourwaybooks.com

Library of Congress Cataloging-in-Publication Data

Prufer, Kevin.
  In a beautiful country / Kevin Prufer.
      p. cm.
    ISBN 978-1-935536-11-6 (pbk. : alk. paper)
    I. Title.
    PS3566.R8I4I6 2011
    811'.54--dc22

                          2010032295

This book is manufactured in the United States of America
and printed on acid-free paper.

Four Way Books is a not-for-profit literary press. We are grateful for the assistance
 we receive from individual donors, public arts agencies, and private foundations.

This publication is made possible with public funds
from the National Endowment for the Arts

and from the New York State Council on the Arts, a state agency.

Distributed by University Press of New England
One Court Street, Lebanon, NH 03766

[clmp]   We are a proud member of the Council of Literary Magazines and Presses.

Contents

In a Beautiful Country   3
Citizen   5
Patriot Missile   7
On Mercy   9

—

Cancer   15
Seeds   18
It Is Not a Star, It Is an Airplane   19
Love Poem   21

—

What I Gave the 20th Century   25
Distant Strangers   26
Behind the Barracks, After the War   28
The New Century   30

—

Love Letter   33
The Internet   34
Love Poem   35
Ars Poetica   36

—

Ars Poetica   39
The Suicides   41
The Ambassador   43
Landscape   46

—

Little Paper Sacrifice   49
Icicles   50
Elegy   52
Burial Hymn in Winter   53

—

God's Grandeur   57
Near Whiteman Air Force Base   58
In Some Parts of the Movie We're Comrades   59
The Villain and His Helicopter   61

—

Late Empires   65
Cartoon Featurette   68
Recent History   69
Broken Statue of Gabriel   71

—

Pre-Elegies   75
Transparent Cities   76
The Failure of Parents to Survive Their Children   80
The Dead Mother   83

—

Four Artes Poeticae   87

—

Night Watch   93
The 20th Century   96
Recent History   97
A Wandering Star   '99

—

Breather   105
Pills   107
In My Brain Is a Room...   108
Postscript   110

In a Beautiful Country

A good way to fall in love
is to turn off the headlights
and drive very fast down dark roads.

Another way to fall in love
is to say they are only mints
and swallow them with a strong drink.

Then it is autumn in the body.
Your hands are cold.
Then it is winter and we are still at war.

The gold-haired girl is singing into your ear
about how we live in a beautiful country.
Snow sifts from the clouds

into your drink. It doesn't matter about the war.
A good way to fall in love
is to close up the garage and turn the engine on,

then down you'll fall through lovely mists
as a body might fall early one morning
from a high window into love. Love,

the broken glass. Love, the scissors
and the water basin. A good way to fall
is with a rope to catch you.

A good way is with something to drink
to help you march forward.
The gold-haired girl says, *Don't worry*

about the armies, says, *We live in a time*
full of love. You're thinking about this too much.
Slow down. Nothing bad will happen.

CITIZEN

Late in the twentieth century
he arrived
             and for many years had nothing
to say.
             Darling, congress told him
from the newspaper, *How we*
                          love you—
before failing into brittleness and pulp.

And his mother dreaming of presidents
while the afternoon showered her with light
until she drowned.
                    And his father
inside of whom the sick vines bloomed—

—

How he grew to love the jets
                          risen from the base
and heavy with bombs.

The crack of flags in stiff winds, the quick
shift
       as the scope finds its target, the click
of metal in the chamber.
                          Or gentler things,
a bee ravishing a flower,
                          the plummet of leaves.

—

The women he'd known and the one he wed
were flowers
               clenching their petals for the night
while the years threw their fame
                              down into his living room.

No germs slipped through his windows,
no ill omen from a far-off shore.
He'd fought in the war
                    and won.
When he died, they put him in a vase.

PATRIOT MISSILE

I loved the half-constructed hulk of it,
the firing condenser that, bared,
                              caught the light
and made of it a copper flare—
                    nose and husk, electrolyte.
And I, tweezing a clot of oil, a metal shaving from its stilled heart,
might smile, as if to tell it *Live*—

—

and it just slept at my work station,
                              its screen gone black and strange,
its alien lungs and chest, in an oiled and armless husk,
its one-eyed head—
                    for days it nearly died in the workroom

—

and I caressed it thusly:
with my thumb across its rough coils, and down
                              where the detonator
clasped the breaker.
              And once, holding its lungs just so, I turned the dial
so the screen came on. It hummed.
                    I told it *Breathe* and, for a moment,
it appeared to. I told it *Darling* and *Love*.

—

And no one in the factory speaks to me.
I've forged a metal face
to cover up my face.
My brain is made of coils, my heart of wires.
I've written down my thoughts and stowed them in its guts
and screwed the breastplate back—

—

Nights, I think about its perfect, absent brain,
the wires that pulse in the breakers,
the payload's hum,
and sometimes wind,
antenna cap and spark, the thought or throb
when it finds its target
and finally smiles.

ON MERCY

Knowing he was soon to be executed
the condemned man asked if first he might

                                          please
have something to drink, if first he might
be drunk.
              So the soldiers brought him a drink
and because there was no hurry, another,
and one for each of them, too.

                                    Soon they were all
very drunk, and this was merciful
because the man probably didn't understand
when they put him to the wall and shot him.

—

I'll marry the man who can prove this happened,
the dying leaves said

                        in their descent.

I'll marry the one who looks through that window,
the waiting grasstips said.

But the sun went on with its golden rays
like a zealous child

and the camera-eyed bees jittered mercifully
in the distant branches.

—

The man slept on the floor
and the little mouse in his head also slept.

The soldiers didn't know who would drag him away
or where they should hide him
so they laughed nervously and one
offered the body a drink, *Ha ha,*
$\qquad\qquad\qquad$ *a toast!*

then left him by the rich lady's liquor cabinet
where she'd find him when she came home from the hills.

——

I'll marry the girl who kisses the lips
and brings a breath to them,
the starving horses said from their fields.

I'll marry the man who pounds the chest
and starts the heart,
$\qquad\qquad\qquad$ the caved-in houses said.

And the window let the light in
until the sun failed in the branches
and, like mercy,
$\qquad\qquad\qquad$ darkness smothered the town.

—

Later in the story, her grown son wrapped him
in a parachute
                    and dumped him in a neighbor's yard.

Later, that neighbor, who understood bad luck,
dragged the man to another's lawn.

And so he traveled, yard to yard,
                              to the edge of town
where at last he slept by a little-traveled road
in a merciful ditch

while the bombers unzipped the sky.

—

And when the town burned, he missed it,
and when the treetops bloomed and charred, he missed it.

I'll marry the man,
the grasstips said in the hot wind,

I'll marry the girl,
the horses said, running from their burning barn, aflame,

their bodies glowing bluely in the dusk.

—

And no one proved it happened,
which was merciful for us all,

the road forgotten, the man gone to root and weed,
to marrow and tooth.

—

And if it had happened—
                    Who would find his jawbone in the loam?
Who would pick out his bullet shells and fillings,
like glitter in the new wood?

And if a man should string them
like words on a golden chain

and make from them a charm,
and give them to his wife,
wouldn't that be mercy, too?

৯

Cancer

A lion almost ate a girl,
                      except her singing calmed it.
She sang about God and his gorgeous mountains,
God and his arms that would lift her
                               from its lair,
until her throat grew raw and her voice gave out
and nothing but the lion
                     could stop her coughing.

—

We have killed all the lions
and who is that who lives in your throat?

It is a tiny woman and she has such a voice
to fill the air with petals—
                     and tiny fingers
that tickle you and make you cough.

—

God in the field over there
                     building trees from the dirt.
God in the woods pasting on flowers.
God crouched on those high branches
                       nudging black clouds
across the sky.

Later, God, his belly full, coughed in his sleep
in the tall grass he'd planted that morning.

—

Unless I misheard him,
the doctor said you had another flower
opening in your throat;
                              its verdurous roots
crept around your heart,
                              down your white arms.
When you exhale,
the room fills with a kind of sweetness
I shouldn't mention.

—

(A petal floated from your lips
and landed on the letter you were writing to me.

Face up to what? It's only a flower.
I can see its roots,
                    green and lovely
beneath the skin on your wrists.)

—

The part about the lion: you were singing to it
and finally it closed its eyes.

Still, you sang
until you knew it slept. Then you lifted its heavy paw
and ran into the woods,
                            and, finding a petal-strewn path,
came home to me.

—

Can't you see this is a love poem?

I printed it out and brought it to you in the hospital
but the doctors,
                    searching for your cough,
had already torn you open,
and there was nowhere for me to sit.

—

Outside, and forty stories down, God
was shaking up the woods
                            so the tall grass swayed
and the wet branches glistened in the rainlight.

—

Petals fell from the lung-like trees.

SEEDS

The pepper on the cutting board and the seeds inside it:
a tiny congregation in a doomed church.

Or the sliced cantaloupe and its stringy heart—
sweet and slick, the closest thing to rot.

I was thinking of you when, distracted, I cut my hand
so blood pearled, then, seed-like, dripped into the sink.

I was thinking of the thick blue vein
where the IV goes.

(Or the mourner who planted his wife beneath his window.
She didn't sprout. She didn't sprout.

Then, one day, an onion shoot,
which he devoured.)

Darling, do not die tonight. The doctors are good,
the hospital quiet as a pill beneath chaff-like stars.

Darling, I brought you flowers and sat by your bed
until the white moon rolled behind the towers.

These days, the faucets won't stop dripping,
and I stand in the kitchen dreaming of nurses

who roam the white halls like quiet animals—
and you, in your bed, unable to call them.

It Is Not a Star, It Is an Airplane

Clouds are a warning,
rain is worse, and next comes lightning

until the birds go quiet
and the dogs start barking.

We were on the phone,
and then a silence—

and I imagined you'd fallen,
the telephone turning above you on its cord.

Such quick bird breaths,
barely audible,

until you came back as if nothing had happened.
Darling, I've been away

too long and my hotel room
is always fresh and strange.

One day I'll be far from home,
and the bird that lives in your heart

might fall from its branch.
Don't say it isn't true.

When I'm worried, I leave the hotel
and walk along the train tracks

where the storm's stopped
and the dogs are no longer barking.

The surgeon said you'd be fine,
patting your arm and looking out the window.

The stars are far away
and, anyway, not interested in us

until one of them moves.
I'm thinking of calling you.

Love Poem

Like you when you're dead, leaves snap from the trees and fall into
the yard.

Like you when you're dead, the thrown newspaper fails to
reach the steps.

Listen! The downed leaves are talking to each other in the wind. So
like you, when you're dead.

It was a warm November day and the absence of snow reminded me
of your condition.

No rain, either. The sun drilling down through the cloudless sky.

On his ladder, a workman was painting away the beautiful wood of
the neighbor's house. *Hello*, I told him

as I walked to my car, which cured like the dead beside the curb.

Then, like you, a train groaned past, setting all the dogs in town to
howling

until, after a while, they had nothing left to tell me.

The silence, then, did little to calm my hands—the scent of rotting leaves, an empty car.

Yesterday, a child was playing in our yard. Now, like you, he's gone. His kite, also, is missing from the sky.

ও

WHAT I GAVE THE 20TH CENTURY

I gave it thirty years. It wanted more.
I loved its mad perambulations
through the outlet malls, its runs
of horror movies and its discount stores.

I poured my thoughts into its internet
and watched them swim like cave-blind carp
milky and quick in the thrilling dark.
Such years and love I gave, in retrospect.

And through it all I had good laughs, and cried
no bitter tears. And as my waistline grew,
so grew my heart. And if a noisy few
enjoyed it less, I say that's sad. I hear they died

and took their dull complaining to the grave.
As for me: I loved it, and I gave.

DISTANT STRANGERS

We received numerous conflicting reports. The dead
numbered many hundreds, thousands,

                                littered the beach,
spilled into the roadway. There were not so many as, at first,
we were led to believe,

                     or else there were far more,
and few survivors walked the smoke-filled streets.
After the accident, earthquakes

                      rattled the emptying houses;
no, it was a factory of unknown utility shuddering into flame.
Or perhaps there were no tremors at all,

                       just distant strangers
fallen that morning or early afternoon,
according to numerous conflicting reports.

—

Late that afternoon, a thick pillar of ash
rose from the island.

                 By dark, the air felt vaguely
acrid to the tongue, a chemical taste I won't soon forget.
The moon turned red and hazy.

                   We heard, then, fewer reports—
an aborted message to a missing lover,

                  the strange clicking
of a transmitter turned off and on
in a pattern no one could decipher.

—

That painting in front of you now
                              I made from memory,
and think I've caught beneath delicate smoke
that rich orange glow of fire consuming the town.
Or here is another
                    you may like better: the black column,
rendered to bisect the canvas, our own fragility
suggested by the ash.
                        Take a catalog, if you'd like,
though the color reproductions
                                can't quite capture
the scope of my enormous project.

Behind the Barracks, After the War

God said, *quit your crying.* God said, *I stopped the planes, I closed the base,*
I turned out the lights, what else do you want?

And down from the mountain, not smoke, but a delicate wind the likes of which
we only half-remembered,

and God said, *I saved some cities, I doused their flames,*

and God said, *I waved away the smoke so you could breathe,*

and on their delicate necks, new flowers swayed in the post-war breeze
so the field smelled sweet and strange,

and *Here is a hand grenade,* God said, *hollow, harmless. Here is a Remington M24,*
bolt-action, also empty—

and it's true the fields stopped burning after a while,

and it's true he had enormous arms,

and, *you live in a free country,* he kept saying, invisible behind the apple tree's
burst of petals,

at ease, he said, *here is your mortar,*

take it home and keep it, here is your nightfighter, here is your interceptor,

take them to your wives, here is your gasmask, here is your repulsion device, here is your pulsebomb, your smartbomb, your brainbomb,

give them to your children, they're useless now,

and then the wind kicked up and then it was late, a cool and lovely evening after the war,

the field behind the barracks exploding with lightning bugs,

my duffel by my side—I was going home at last—and, *what's wrong with you?*

God said from high above the rooftop. *Cheer up!*

THE NEW CENTURY

Don't get up, don't give me that talk about I'm sorry
and Look at the woods how beautiful the woods are
when the snow flits through those holes I punched in the treetops,
said God.
                    God said, I don't care if your knees get muddy,
I don't care if your dinner burns,
                                        and while he spoke
the new century crept up behind me so I could hear
twigs snap,
                and God said, Don't turn around, and I don't care
if your house burns, I will part the treetops with these big hands
so I can watch, I will fan the flames with barn doors
and while he spoke
                        the new century was touching
the back of my neck with tiny fingers, was playing
just beyond my sight,
                        and God said, Don't look around,
don't get up, don't praise the winter sunset over the far-off
mountains because I don't care if your wife, your child, catch fire,
haven't you been paying attention?
                                    And from behind me
the new century was laughing not like a child,
but like a rusted old wheel
                    spinning.

ఎ

LOVE LETTER

I wish you were in my time zone. Illinois or Arkansas
will do. I have eaten the peach
down to the hard stone. The rain
has flattened a yellow leaf to the window. Is it dark yet
where you are? Here the news comes
waterlogged and smeared to the driveway. The sky greens
and the grass tips bend like damp old ladies
searching for coins. Someone is whispering
in the trees—someone,
eyes wrapped in yellow leaves, says something
I don't understand.

THE INTERNET

If it is dead when you read this poem
remember its many grassy ways,

its empty spaces filling with light.
It had such trees and lace-like roots,

such pools where ideas turned,
where its brain floated in broth.

I drank
until stars fell from the clouds.

Winter brought networks of static
from the curved glass sky,

the circuitry of ice on water,
snow deleting the fields.

I loved it so much
I couldn't catch my breath.

If it has outlived me,
sit beneath its endless branches

and think of my empty mouth
turning to granite.

LOVE POEM

I'll make you a bomb. First the booster gas canister,
then the heat shield, then the radium case, which, yes,
is shaped like a peanut. I'll make you a bomb,
first the heat field, then the lenses that drive
the implosion, and last the radiation space, which,
yes, is shaped like a peanut. I'll make you a bomb,
first the space filler, then the glass lenses,
which, careful, may implode. I'll make you a swan,
first a crease here, then a crease there, a quick tuck
for the wings, an explosion of flight. I'll make you a swan,
one-two-three folds and now it's done, but it will not fly,
its wing tips burning like fuses. I'll make you a dress,
don't you love me? a nip and a tuck and three pins
to hold it tight. I'll make you a little white dress,
inside it your heart says *bang, bang, bang*, your mind
like a swan's. Careful, it's shaped like a peanut,
careful of when it decays, careful, it may implode.
Don't you love me? Look what I've made you.

ARS POETICA

A bomb undid the barn
and blew the horse apart
and charred the little lamb
I loved with half my heart.
(It made me think of art.)

Another caught my neighbors
laughing by the stairs.
And how their house was cinders,
and how their bodies flared!
(A poem was burning there.)

The artist's mind does well
to look on human ill
and find in it some beauty,
God's bright material
(and thanks for those who fail).

It was a kindly God
who tore the town apart.
Very kindly, He
who held my punctured heart.
(Its ink was thick and dark.)

79451102

(Amazon order #102-8825904-2614636)

Date ordered: 2013-03-20 20:32:38 - *Ship via:*Standard

In a Beautiful Count...

Z-PG-00964

1935536117 QTY: 1

Release your orders

BORDERS®

Returns

Returns of merchandise purchased from a Borders, Borders Express or Waldenbooks retail store will be permitted only if presented in saleable condition accompanied by the original sales receipt or Borders gift receipt within the time periods specified below. Returns accompanied by the original sales receipt must be made within 30 days of purchase and the purchase price will be refunded in the same form as the original purchase. Returns accompanied by the original Borders gift receipt must be made within 60 days of purchase and the purchase price will be refunded in the form of a return gift card.

Exchanges of opened audio books, music, videos, video games, software and electronics will be permitted subject to the same time periods and receipt requirements as above and can be made for the same item only.

Periodicals, newspapers, comic books, food and drink, eBooks and other digital downloads, gift cards, return gift cards, items marked "non-returnable," "final sale" or the like and out-of-print, collectible or pre-owned items cannot be returned or exchanged.

Returns and exchanges to a Borders, Borders Express or Waldenbooks retail store of merchandise purchased from Borders.com may be permitted in certain circumstances. See Borders.com for details.

ARS POETICA

Just before he walked through the patio door, it started to snow.

Down the great flakes fell, over the birdbath, over the mailbox. Over the children playing next door.

He'd heard the phone ring and knew exactly who it was. He'd been waiting.

Big wet snowflakes decorated the dog asleep beside the grill. And the evening's red light glinting off the glass doors—

he didn't notice the patio doors were shut. He walked right on through so the glass shattered around him.

The phone kept ringing as glass slid from its frame into his arms, as it bit into his shoulder, his neck.

The phone was saying, *Here I am! Here I am!*

And every snowflake tried to hold out another moment in the warm grass.

He stood on the threshold, looking at the black phone as if he could reach it. Then he touched his neck, where more glass was.

The phone had a little silver heart that was singing, singing!

And outside, the neighbors were saying to each other, *Will you look at that? Spring already, and snow!*

Having plucked a tooth of glass from his neck, the man, too, was nearly asleep.

And where was I? There I was, on the other side of town, looking out the window at the snow,

holding this brand new poem in one hand and my phone in the other.

THE SUICIDES

The girls were dying all over the lawn,
                      their white skirts blown
and flapping in the breeze, a whisper
                      of nylon or newly set hair
as the air went red and the winds grew chill.

—

Then the pink sun fell
                and cooled behind the trees,
the lawn grown strange in the sunset's blare,
the dead girls—leaves caught and rustling in their hair—

—

A blush crept down their throats,
and curled and faded there. Their lips turned gray
and grayer still.
               Their bodies seemed to fade away.

—

When darkness finally fell
              like a winding cloth—
when I couldn't see the suicides in the pitch—I felt
much better. They had such sad faces.
                    It's always hard to look—

—

(the frown that remains when the head's an empty space,
the swollen lips,

the eyes in the porch light's glare)

—

—even though there's no longer

real sadness there.

The Ambassador

I came to that place where the road split
and I saw it was a settlement,

                      so I told the natives:
Citizens, I have brought you marvelous things
and *I come from far away and ask just this of you*
—until an arrow struck me in the chest

                            and down I fell

into a wheelrut.

—

They stole my coins and made of them a necklace.
They took my shoes and wore them wrongly.
I slept in a tangle of roots,

                felt snow cap that bit of skull
that, open to the weather, chilled and ached my quiet head.
(Our capitol was warmer, and far too far away,
and when I closed my eye

                I could recall it

—

draped across the hills like sleepy women.)

                       Rootwork,
loam, a trill of woodbugs undid my arms and back,
and now and then the rattle

                of a clumsy native wagon

passed me by and never stopped.
My shoulders popped and came unsocketed,
and still the thought of lights

—

                              along the avenues
was a comfort in the seasons, even as increasing
traffic leveled the road beside me.
                              And thus I sank
and faded deeper into dirt,

where no one stole my shinbone and cut from it a comb,
where no one saw my glass eye and thought it was a jewel.

—

In darkness, the mind
                    is a nimbler thing, and strange.
From footsteps and the noise of wheels, I made up stories:
A war and then my city lost in a fire.
                              A crying nymph—for years
I heard her in the whirr of spinning tires—
                              as up her nightgown
flames like curious fingers crept.
                              The thud of engines
and the cries of dying, dark-skinned men—

—

                                        all are fancy and,
as such, are voids. I am a worthless, unproductive thing,
far beneath the weeds:
                        jawbone split by roots, a useless finger bone,
while natives turn the earth above and, once or twice,
a piece of me turns with it,
                        rising to catch the air,
then down again into the soil.

LANDSCAPE

On a spring day,
where the road from the hospital
becomes gravel then dirt,
an old man chops wood.
His dog no longer lifts his ears
with each swing of the axe.
It has rained a little
and the old man works hard,
the wood splintering in pieces.
Someone has hung a cow's head
from a nearby fence post. Someone
has stripped all the feathers
from that bird. The dog
is very old and has three legs.
In another poem, he will bound
from the porch into the woods
where he will cease to exist.
The old man raises his axe.
The dog's stump twitches in a dream.
The hospital, too, is sleeping on its hill,
having eaten well of us.
It is a beautiful, blue, spring day
after a cool rain. And look,
I am no longer even human.
I have obliterated myself.

৯

LITTLE PAPER SACRIFICE

First a fold here, then a cut there and now it's an angel
with little holes for eyes.

I'd give it to you, but you have so many.

First a cut here, then a cut there and now it's a ghost.
That little emptiness is its mouth.

I'd give it to you, but I know how you feel
about snipped-off wings.

But look—a few quick cuts to give it arms and legs
and he's a perfect little man.

I'd give him to you, but he cannot cry from those holes,
I'd give him to you, but he still needs teeth.

But look—one across the middle, another there,
and he's just trousers and a shirt.

I'll draw in buttons, if you like. I'll draw a collar.

Will you wear them if they fit?
I'd give you the scissors, but I'm afraid of what you'll do.

ICICLES

The light from my neighbor's computer
cast the half-melted snow

in a queer blue light.

—

Melting icicles remind me
of a hospital

where, suspended from a pole,
a plastic bag

drips into your arm.

—

And my neighbors were hunched at their screens,
like nothing had happened,

emailing each other
about the weather.

—

Sometimes, my heart is a half-filled bag,
draining slowly

into the evening.

—

Listening closely, I heard the tap-tap
of my neighbors at their keyboards,

icicles dripping.

A thousand icicles
long as the night.

—

And from my heart, tubes descend.
Lower and lower, they branch and thin.

The last of my blood
empties into them.

ELEGY

Where did you go, dear bruised,

                           dear slack,

then posthumous—

                 then elusive and coy?

Were you a naughty boy,

                    so sent down the stairs

to flap your wings

               in the basement's dark?

Did they plug you in

                so you'd tick or spark?

Did friends crowd your sickroom,

                   your face

like a clock's. [A blip on your screen, a tear

                           from the scared.]

Dear love, dear gone,

             did they put you in a box

and the box into the earth

               where you mucked like a child

among roots and grubs? [Here is the part

                  where it rains;

this is the thunder that helps you sprout.]

                  Dear strange,

dear leaf—

       will a hand come down and pluck you out?

Burial Hymn in Winter

I drifted among crowds
until my heart said *no,*
and they put me in a box
and the box into the snow.

In the all-repressing snow
I slept a hundred days.
The wind caressed the fields.
My skin went tough and gray.

And when the ground unfroze,
they lowered me into soil.
The tilting of my bones
made me think of seas.

Instead of a box, a ship
might float me far from home.
Instead of sky to fix a course,
the skull's black arc of bone.

The unmoored mind does well
to complicate the dark.
I listed thus on freezing seas
and didn't see the shore—

until a root thrust through the soil
and split my slats apart.
Until it fingered past my shirt
for the water in my heart—

GOD'S GRANDEUR

Drink up, drink up, the girls behind the bar were saying, pretty
and sorry-eyed.
                        And outside, exurban three-a.m., a three-a.m.
of new housing and its treeless acres, three-a.m. of mountains
invisible in the dark,
                        streetlamps and the thoughtless schoolyards
of someone else's youth.
                        Drink up, the wet-lipped girls kept saying,
and night lay like a sleeping woman on the highway,
tuneless night, loveless night—
                        Drink up, and the stars
like twirling hubcaps, the stars like sprung glass, shattered
where the head went through.
                        I had had too much to drink
and was harmless now to the girls who said *Drink up*
and smiled and I drank up.
                        And how could I not think of you,
dead these years, beneath the unaverted, receding stars?

57

NEAR WHITEMAN AIR FORCE BASE

The phone is always ringing *America!*
And the lawnmowers say *America!* chopping up the yards.
And church bells: sometimes they say *America!*
and sometimes they say *Jesus!* It's hard to tell,
their clappers swaying on chains like hanged men.

And all along Broad Street, boys idle in pick-ups
while a spring rain dots their windshields
with a million tiny bombs. The windshields
smear over and the girls giggle *America!*
until the lights turn green and off they go.

It is so beautiful in my town after rain, wet leaves
clogging up the drains, that hint of decay.
And when the sun falls behind the steeple,
it says *So long, America!* And when the bombers
rise from the night-lit base, they say *Hello, children!*

IN SOME PARTS OF THE MOVIE WE'RE COMRADES

In some parts of the movie we're comrades and friendly, we're half-drunk and youthful.

In some parts of the movie, it's Saigon or Baghdad, dark streets and lonesome. Oh vacant-eyed natives, thick-tongued and eerie, wired-in-the-jackets. [Cue music, cue chatter.]

In some we're outnumbered. Did you hear that? An enemy footfall. A whistle, as if from afar; another, and closer, vague in the moonlight. One comrade already dead. [Cue crickets. Cue windsong through reeds.]

In others: loud bombers. In some prints: the glamour of flares and of tracers. Sometimes, such music! Always, the parachutes—opened like palms or blooms.

We have a comrade who's sad, who misses his new wife back home. She writes him such letters, he shows us. [A click in the grass and he's dead.]

[Cut to sad mountains. Cut to the heavens where God lives.]

Some parts are hand-held and some parts are night-lit—so we're grainy, the camera keeps bouncing, unnerving. The hostiles approach us. You twist the black wire to the red one. The bomb holds its breath.

Our comrade keeps lookout. [Then later he's dead.]

Then: fire. The village is burning. Then: music, uplifting and vatic. [Cue fireworks, cue powder.] How lovely our faces,

and perfect, the gape-mouthed, the blown into ribbons and dying, fantastic. And then from the rubble, just us and those rooftops collapsing.

Just us, we're approaching the camera, sweat-streaked and panting, battered and smiling. Behind us, the village keeps burning. [Our comrade is charring?] [Cue credits.] More rockets, more airplanes! More bullets! [Roll credits.] Such acting!

In some parts, the audience loves us to pieces.

THE VILLAIN AND HIS HELICOPTER: POSSIBLE MOVIE RENTAL VERSIONS

In the simple, VHS version
the blasted helicopter
falls into the sea
and disappears just before
the credits scroll
the picture away. On DVD
a commotion in the pod
is visible, the rotors
scurling up smoke, the helicopter
tilting dangerously into
the sea. In the Digit-L Letterbox
Limited Release, the villain presses
his white face to the glass
and groans, the helicopter's
rotors grinding and coughing
smoke. In the Director's Cut
you can hear the sound his fingers make
against the glass, like little
suction cups. In D-Lux
Dolby Stereo, the engine
dies in slow motion, every
gear grinding away,
the villain mouthing these words:
tell my wife ... my son ...
In the Premier Unrated DVD
you can just discern a flashback
to the villain's past, his mother
singing him to sleep.
In the Wide-Screen, Criterion Edition

a single tear streaks his flushed cheek
as the helicopter smiles,
like any good machine,
into the senseless, reflecting sea.

❀

LATE EMPIRES
a dead girl by the road

Like a stadium,
                    emptying its hushed crowds—
Like a fallen empire, spilling refugees—
the stomach
                    displays its contents.

——

Sorry, the grass said
                    to the fingers' rigid purple,
to the half-smile where an arm bone
cracked
                    and split the skin. *Sorry*,
to the face on the roadside, to the gravel
pitted in the flesh

——

that has sunk these last weeks
into the scrub,

that has cooled in the mists,
the clouds
                    of drunken flies.

——

He is far away
                    sleeping on a hotel bed,
singing to the radio,

driving to the city
with another girl
                    for drinks, more drinks.
We'll have a drink, he says.

—

Rome fell;
the girl fell when he hit her hard.

The girl cried out
and, like Rome, fell on her broken arm
on the roadside.

The girl cried in the sun
on the gravel,
                    and a knife
to the baths, a knife to the libraries,
knife to the Palatine, knife to the slums,
knife to the throat
                         that wanted only
to keep its voice inside it.

—

The silence between one Rome
and another:
             each empire's incipient failure,
a body's slow decay.
                 He has already forgotten,
he is far away, and, anyway, this is only
a dead girl,
             having spilled a population
into the grass.

CARTOON FEATURETTE

I saw you tumble from the roof.
It broke your head in two.
Stars and robins spun around
the doubleness of you.

Your right eye looked up to the clouds
where God was roused from sleep.
And in the background, music swelled
and made the angels weep.

Your other eye was just an X,
a cancellation mark.
It blotted out the clouds and yard
and filled the sky with dark.

But as my eyes adjusted,
I came to see the truth—
This was a darkened theatre
and high up in his booth

the projectionist had gone to sleep.
A reel was spinning there,
its loose end flapping as it churned
the warming, dust-filled air.

Recent History

He didn't notice that they'd drained the pool.

The song of power mowers, the thrum of bees, the delicate necks of flowers—

He didn't notice that they'd drained the pool and up he climbed, a little drunk, and waved to us from the topmost rung.

There was a war on, but it was far away. A breath of newspapers in the summer winds—

We called to him and waved our arms. He didn't notice

as evening approached, its half-dark breezes, grass-scented and queer. Then he waved back, smiling.

There was a war on and he wore blue shorts and a funny hat, standing at the high dive's lip like it was a show,

the bees accosting the quickly closing flowers, a gasp of papers, the power mower's spinning blade.

No, we cried, and *Don't*. He laughed and waved his arms, feigned drunk. He'd had too much to drink

and so had we. At the bottoms of our glasses, little slugs of ice.

Then he bounced once and rose into the evening air, where, for the loveliest moment, at the top of his arc,

(and we often retold this as the war went forward)

he finally noticed the empty pool and, startled, seemed to understand

the source of our objections.

Broken Statue of Gabriel

Carla said it was a body in the snow.
                    I told her, *no,*
a play of shadow, a discarded coat
and *cold place for a nap,*
                    ha ha. And the complicated snow
came down like parachutes over the city's towers,
freezing cars, lamp posts,
                    the boy we found
asleep in the drift,

—

                    his intricate wings tucked beneath his back,
his veined, webbed fingers. White-cheeked and strange—
                                        snow
that kissed his forehead, and the single flake
that clung, a moment, to an eyelash, then wouldn't disappear.
Lips gone chill, gone gray as winter weather
                                and the wind detached
a single feather, tossing it
                    down the snow-encrusted street.

—

And Carla leaned over him, touched the cheek, and smiled—
he's beautiful—
                    And in the wind he seemed to breathe.
I told her *he's ok* and *let him sleep it off.*

71

                    The fingers moved—
it may have been the wind again—and Carla didn't budge,
so I said I'd call the cops to haul the thing away.

—

Soon we'd drawn a crowd of sad-faced girls
leaving the bars for the night; old men,

                              a few of whom began to weep.
Someone said he had the perfect body of a soldier.
He held a shield and someone said he must have lost his sword.
He's like a picture in a book,
                    Carla whispered, not to me.
And then we saw the cruiser's warm red light,

                              steady as an artery,

pulsing around the corner.

৶

PRE-ELEGIES

And what have you got now? A mother? Father?
Voices that pulse through the lines then falter,
the phone's emptying heart? They say they love you,
but now they are hanging up. Early day, things to do
tomorrow. And now they are maybe lying
in bed with their magazines, now they are talking
about someone else, no one you know.
Lights out, now—it's late, and they've grown old.

But both are still alive, and that's good luck.
They've drifted along with their lives just
as you have let yours drift. And here you are, alone,
half drunk on the couch, cradling your phone.
The dark outside is gentle and insistent:
Best to lose them slowly to their distance.

Transparent Cities

I fell into a snow bank and didn't wake again,
but felt, in my few moments that remained,
                                        the flush of childhood,
and saw (until my eyeballs bleared and wouldn't close)
                                                the snow
like angels over me—
                        windswirl and gasp,
in every hand a needle—and then the sting as my dull flesh
chilled and wouldn't pulse again.
                                Next morning
they hauled me out and threw me in a wagon.

—

                                        Familiar city
that fills me with confetti, that thrills my hair. Lines of gas lights,
lines of girls—
        A painless way to go,
you know? I think the driver said. *The body falls asleep.*

Terrible city many years from now
                                and the burning paper
that sears the hair with embers—

—

                                I slept under awnings
and snow drifts, drunk—
                then woke in a wagon,

gifted with a kind of sight I hadn't had before.
I saw the streets give way before me
to illumination, glare, a swarm
                                of buses and the feline hum
of well-lit storefronts.
                        Falls of light confused my eyes.

—

And *He's such a gentle boy,* my mother used to say.

—

And *Pity he had to die like that, the fool*—from far away,
the voice that drove the corpse wagon.
                                His friend just laughed
and down the early morning street
                        the black horse pulled us on.

—

How strange the city
                my city would become
and though my fingers ached and wouldn't move—
and though my body never thawed—I rocked with every step
the black horse took
                and gasped to see transparent towers rise
like God's great hands unflexing from the snow banks,

—

and quivered at the lights that dressed them all in gems,
a young man falling

from among them.

—

And *Fairy dust*,

my mother called it in a story years ago—
She turned the page: a princess dozed in bed,
the sweet half-blush that traced her spellbound throat,

and vines

overgrowing the windowpanes. *One more page*, she said,
then off to bed with you.

—

Such buildings and the dust

that glittered over us.

—

And so the princess slept a thousand years—
The wagon creaked, its axles stiff with cold
as we pulled up to the city morgue.
Snow sifted from above

and still I wanted more.

—

My mother must have turned the page
as down the buildings fell
                              into glitter and crash,
and down the city tumbled
into perfect banks of ash.

The Failure of Parents to Survive Their Children

The moon burned all night long

                            so by morning it had shrunk,

and glowed like a coal in the sky.

—

Its sparks had set the trees afire.

You said you'd rest awhile beneath them
until you disappeared

                   in the burning, falling leaves.

—

You were my father, then I changed your name.
You were my mother

                until she, too, passed.

——

You were burning so thoughtfully in the field

                          like a horse who,

running from a flaming barn, himself engulfed in flame,
sets the grass afire

              as he passes through it.

—

Look, my brother said, meaning the dead man
covered with the remains of leaves.

When we brushed the char and soot away,
we saw that he was beautiful—
                              dark hair and eyes white as aspirin.

——

Like a memory of loved ones, the moon smoked all night long
until it no longer resembled itself.

——

                              And showers of ashes—
from the sky and the trees. All the rooftops on fire
and soot to fill the wheelruts,
                              to black our faces—

——

Look, my brother said, meaning—

——

*(I thought I saw my parents silhouetted against the barnfire in the night,
two gasps against the treefire. Moonfire.)*

——

81

—meaning the body
buried in the black char of branches
that was, after all, not a man, but a woman,
that was, after all,
a pile of leaves—

THE DEAD MOTHER

What you call dying I call sleeping
so snow covered my windows and wind rocked the gurney.

Shuffle and hush, a gasp
                         from the breath machine, and soon
I knew I'd be away from there,
soon, the light would turn the roofs to glitter. The flags to colors.

—

Where I'm writing from, you cannot reach.
Where I'm writing from, you have to sleep. I mean,
                               you have to die.

And all night, the angels of commerce drift earthwards,
white gowns you'd call dove-like,
                         chalk-like. The pills of snow.
Blood cells—

—

         We're not old women here,
neither addled nor forgetful anymore. Mornings
the mall opens its arms to us, an electric hiss
                         of doors, a rush
of heat, and such gold and fabrics as I have never seen

until my breath goes ragged and my heart grows dim.

83

—

And a coin rises over America to fill the glass with light
and nearly melts the snow.
                              And escalators lift us higher
through the many-windowed mall, past glassware.
                                                  Past tiers
of dishes, wintergear, and speakers—

—

My brain was a lily, its lips pursed nearly closed—
then you kissed me in the hospital and said *Hello.*
                                          You held my hand
and asked the doctors: *Can she hear me?* I had almost gone
by then, but liked your voice,
                          which came to me as if from far away,

—

and follows still,
                higher up the escalators to the farthest, glassed-in floors.
And through the window, a field of lovely cars,
                                        a moneyed sky,
our empty house, the highway dropping toward the river.

Four Artes Poeticae

I

At the center of every onion,
a translucent eye

turns in its socket
but cannot see.

When I planted one in the empty yard,
a stalk shot up

to attract the hungry deer.
Below ground, that little eye

kept spinning,
bloodshot and enraged.

2

Dear God of Art,
I was always talking to you.

When I thought you answered
my heart rustled behind my ribs

like a giant insect
in a cage.

I had to feed it something.
I transcribed everything you said

on squares of paper
which, later, I devoured.

3

I dissected your butterfly
and found inside

a heart like a watch spring.
It had a strange escapement

cast in gold.
I made from that the chain

I'm wearing now.
Can't you hear me?

I left the wings on the cutting board
thinking you'd admire them.

4

From the kitchen window,
I watched your hundred deer

eat the leaves and the branches,
the flowers and the onion shoot.

When there was nothing left,
they walked away.

I kept chopping,
not realizing I'd cut my finger.

The yard was like an empty page again.
A little ink pulsed out.

৵

NIGHT WATCH

A man was driving past the hospital with his son
when he felt a fluttering in his chest
which at first he took for nerves, because it was snowing
very hard and his young son was cranky
and squirming and how could he possibly see the road
with all this weather?
                    Then his hand began
to hurt, and then his wrist and arm,
so he pulled to the side of the road,
where, moments later, he died.

—

And the snow fell like angels,
                         and the boy watched
them cover the windows. Such snow
he had never seen, his father
asleep beside him, snow sifting
over the hush of the city and the car,
which grew darker,
                    dark as his room at night
and quiet, buried in snow.
                    And soon, he, too,
was asleep. And soon, the engine died.

—

I made up this story
                    sitting beside my father's bed.
Outside the hospital,
                    it had begun to snow,
capping the cars twenty stories down.
And the liquid in his lungs,
                              the drip and its clear tube,
the nurses lost to their machines and trays,
the sun long set—
                    in a whirl of snow, I hoped,
the brain goes dim and cold, a hush of snow
when the breathing stops
and the heart beats on
                    for a minute or so—

—

And all night long, cars swooped past the hospital,
headlights and wipers,
                        men hunched in their cockpits
through the blinding snow toward home.
The high window
                    looked over the freeway
where the child in my story slept in his father's car,
his face grown cold and his fingers numb.
And all night, silent nurses
                              swept past the room
where I kept my watch.

—

And the cops wiped snow from the window
with their fists. They rapped on the glass,
but no one moved. They knocked a little harder,
then tried the door,
                    which was frozen shut.
My father, as I implied, would die that night.
That was thirty days ago.
                        And the boy,
he was far below, in a story I invented,
sleeping in a car
                as daylight broke through clouds,
and try as they might,
                    they couldn't wake him.

The 20th Century

Kiss its cheek, then smooth its sad, gray hair.
Bring it secret cigarettes. How could they hurt
it anymore? A smoke to stanch the fear
is mercy in the end. The doctors purse

their lips or look away. They occupy their hands
with clipboards. Leave them to their notes. Smile. It's what
the dying want. Not tears, you fool. Nor bland-
eyed sentiment. Truth, neither. Offer it

a light. Tell that joke about the Jew, the queer,
the drunken nigger. There you go. It smiles
at that, and so should you. Nothing quells our fears
like comedy, nothing sublimates our ills—

And if it finds no comfort from your visit,
put a pillow to its mouth, and, so, be done with it.

Recent History

All night, angels
                 crashed through the trees,
so the yard was a scatter
                    of bent, failing bodies.
You said: *Another!* to the crackling of branches.
Their scraps are so sweet where they sway with the leaves.

—

From the garden, the asters said: *Love was their weakness.*
The firefly's bright little heart disagreed.

Then down fell another, where it cracked on a low branch,
waking the neighbors
                  who leaned from their windows
and peered toward the trees.

—

A crowd had collected
                   in bathrobes and nightgowns,
their faces lit greenly in the angels' dim glow.
I'd like to have known them
                  when they were more vibrant,
you said, looking down,

—

where one gurgled strangely,

                          its wings come undone.
A child had collected a handful of feathers.
Another threw sticks

                    at one caught on a limb.
We'd better get digging, our neighbor said softly.
They'll stink in the sun.

A WANDERING STAR

It was thin as a scratch on the skin
that later swelled
                and flushed.
Then brighter, all week, it grew:
                            a glare and burst.
It glowed like an airplane
                  trailing flame—
And closer, ever day, it came.

—

You lay in your bed. I said,
                Dad, come see!
But you were far too sick.
              I said, *Look!*
You groaned and turned
and waved me away.
               By now, it far outshone
the sun
        and below our windows people milled
and squinted at the sky.

—

The room grew warm,
             so I closed the blinds.
You lay in your bed where I brought you soup,

you skin gone slack,
                    mottled and thin.

The doctor never came,
and I knew—but I didn't want to say—

In the sky the new sun
                    flowered and glowed.

—

When the treetops burst in flame,
                              I prayed,
but I didn't leave your side. When the rooftops
charred,
        you said, *Go to the cellar and leave me here.*
But I stayed. Light
burned through the blinds
while I stroked your head.
                              You sighed,
then failed in the heat.

—

When I woke, the star had turned,
had swung on its orbit away.
                              The room had dimmed

and I heard people cheer in the street
where they picked at the char

                          and the ruins
or pointed to the sky, relieved.

—

Still, we had two suns for months.
The air stayed warm

                    and at night
I watched the far-off hayfields burn,
caught their scent

                    when the hot winds
blew from the hills. But the star grew
dimmer every day,
until at last, like you,

                        it blinked away.

৯

BREATHER

The heart attack
ought to learn to relax,
ought to worry less
about distant places.
The heart attack
ought to take a walk
in the evening's cool,
stroll around the block
and clear his head.
Here uptown, everyone's
curled in bed or fresh
from the bath.
Breathe, breathe,
says the heart attack,
look at the houses and take
a long breath. How fresh
the air is late at night,
it dries the sweat.
Downtown's a mess
of noise and blacks,
and farther still
someone flicks a switch
someone puts a match
to a twisting fuse.
But here, the heart attack
has friends, here the air
is cool. Here he can take

himself around the block
and up his steps, can lock
his door and relax,
can wrap himself snug
in electric blankets.

PILLS

The pills of morning and the pills of night
were lost in conversation on the bedside table.
The former said, *He's only sleeping late*;
The latter congregation thought it right

to note his open eyes, point out the window
and its squares of morning light.
The old cat, long asleep across his toes,
found them now unyielding, yawned, rose

and slipped into the kitchen for its food.
From the dresser, the same old clock said,
Rise! Rise! He never moved,
while day revised the morning and night improved

on day. His eyes dried out, his cheeks began to sink,
and the pills of morning on the bedside table
said, *He hasn't moved! He's tired for goodness sake!*
The pills of night replied: *He's wide awake.*

In My Brain Is a Room; In That Room You Are Sleepin

It's not the worst thing about murder
That it is utter blasphemy.

—Elena Fanailova

The sad thing about murder
is the window left open,

                        the cut screen,

the rain that stains your carpet,
a gathering pool—

—

He kept washing his hands.
Then he sat in the corner and smoked.
When he heard a car pull into the drive

                              he climbed out the window

and walked calmly down the road.

—

You couldn't

               cry out, couldn't unknot your arms.

The sad thing was,

               what arms?

The sad thing was the garage door opening,
the familiar voice in the hall: *I'm home!*

—

Love the long night of the mind,

                              love the half-remembered
sweetness of doors opening, the cooling mind,
the brain that seemed, at first, to spin
                              on its stem and now
just sleeps.

——

I am inventing this story on a quiet night in an empty house
in the rural Midwest.
                    Outside: rain to wash his tracks away.

——

I am inventing this story because I live in God's country
and his million glass stars
                        keep falling
on the rooftop.

——

In my brain, a little door slides open.
                        Here is a room.
In the room, a doll-like woman has died. And then
it gets brighter, brighter.
                    The storm must be lifting
behind the tiny windows.

POSTSCRIPT

Here is my receipt for the paper.
Thank you. It snowed the whole way to the store,
which was crowded with secretaries. Thank you
for reimbursing me for my expenses.

Here is my receipt for the pencils.
Now you will have something to write with.
It's still snowing, but I don't mind.
The secretaries at the store were warming their hands
on cups of coffee.

I could file those for you, would you like that?
I could clip them in nicely with the three-hole-punch.
You shouldn't have to worry about little things,
what with the snow falling like secretaries.

What with the snow falling like a million poems.
I could gather them for you, clip them into the three-ring binders.
And don't you love the lines of secretaries
trudging down the street with their bags and coffee?

Yes, I guess it's been a long day. I'm a little tired,
yes. The secretaries falling from the sky like cut-out angels
were just too much. So many wings cluttering the avenue.
Here are the poems I have gathered
and this is the receipt.

Acknowledgments

These poems appeared previously, often in somewhat different forms, in the following journals:

AGNI, American Poetry Review, Barrow Street, Black Warrior Review, Colorado Review, Crazyhorse, Field, Flatmancrooked, The Georgia Review, Hayden's Ferry Review, Indiana Review, The Kenyon Review, The Laurel Review, The New England Review, New Orleans Review, The New Republic, Opium, Ploughshares, Poetry, Prairie Schooner, Redivider, River Styx, Shenandoah, Southwest Review, Subtropics, 32 Poems, Virginia Quarterly Review.

"On Mercy" was reprinted in *Best American Poetry 2009.*

"Breather" borrows music from Frederick Seidel's "Grandson Born Dead." The poem "Little Paper Sacrifice" is for Laura Jensen, whose work inspired it. "Love Poem," also, is inspired by the work of Laura Jensen. "Behind the Barracks, After the War" was written for Rachel Zucker and Arielle Greenberg's blog *Starting Today: Poems for the First 100 Days.* It was reprinted in the anthology of the same title.

Thanks especially to Sally Ball, Joy Katz, John Gallaher, Wayne Miller, and R. M. Kinder for their editorial help. And to Martha Rhodes for her faith in my work. This book is for Mary.

Kevin Prufer is the author of four previous poetry collections, the most recent of which, *National Anthem*, was named one of the five best poetry books of 2008 by *Publishers Weekly*. He's also editor of *New European Poets* and *New Young American Poets*, and Editor-at-Large of *Pleiades: A Journal of New Writing*. The recipient of fellowships from the National Endowment for the Arts and the Lannan Foundation, he teaches at the University of Houston.